ISBN 0 947338 37 3

This edition published 1994 exclusively for Selecta Book Ltd,
Folly Road, Roundway, Devizes, Wiltshire, UK.

Romantic Roses

Photographs:

Graham McGeagh

David Sinclair

The rose that all are praising,
Is not the rose for me,
Too many eyes are gazing
Upon the faultless tree.
But there's a rose in yonder glen
That scorns the gaze of other men;
For me its beauty saving,
Oh! that's the rose for me.

T.H. BAYLY

Four Seasons

I know a little garden close
Set thick with lily and red rose,
Where I would wander if I might
From dewy dawn to dewy night,
And have one with me wandering.

WILLIAM MORRIS

Scuts Briar

Who ever called a rose a rose
Aptly named it, as it grows
So lovely with its colours rare,
Its sweet perfume which fills the air.
'A rose by any other name'
they say -
I close my eyes, but come what
may
No other name comes to my mind,
Because I know I'll only find
A rose can only be a Rose.

B.M.M.

Pinkie

I put my question to the flower:
'Pride of the summer,
garden Queen,
Why livest thou thy little hour?'
And the rose answered,
'I am seen.'

I put my question to the root.
'I mine the earth content,'
it said,
'A hidden minor underfoot:
I know a rose is overhead'

JOHN JAMES PIATT

Baron E de Rothschild

More exquisite
than any other
is the autumn rose.

THEODORE D'AUBIGNE

Happy Event

What's in a name?
that which we call a rose
By any other name
would smell as sweet.

WILLIAM SHAKESPEARE

From fairest creatures we
desire increase
That thereby beauty's rose
might never die.

WILLIAM SHAKESPEARE

Four Seasons

'Tis the last rose of summer
Left blooming alone;
All her lovely companions
Are faded and gone.

JULIA A. MOORE

Peace

Red Rose, proud Rose,
sad Rose of all my days!
Come near me,
while I sing the ancient ways.

W.B.YEATS

Papa Meilland

But never yet, by night or day,
In dew of spring, or summer's ray,
Did the sweet Valley shine so gay
As now it shines, all love and light,
Visions by day, and feasts by night!
A happier smile illumes each brow,
With quicker spread each heart uncloses,
And all is ecstacy, - for now
The Valley holds its Feast of Roses.

MOORE

Buff Beauty

This world that we're livin' in
Is mighty hard to beat;
You git a thorn with every Rose
But ain't the Roses sweet.

FRANK L STANTON

Iceberg

Gather ye rose buds while ye may,
Old Time is still a-flying;
And this same Rose that smile today,
Tomorrow will be dying,
Then be not coy, but use your time;
And while ye may, go marry:
For having lost but once your prime,
You may forever tarry.

ROBERT HERRICK

Kalinka

The Rose

I came upon a flower
So sweet, so pure,
Its beauty so exquisite
It filled my heart with joy,
Enthralled I stood and gazed
I could not pass it by
Perfection such as this
Deserved more than a glance.
Its petals shone with dew
Like tears about to fall,
Oh Queen of all the flowers
It was a lovely rose.

DOROTHY LOCKETT

Dainty Bess

The red rose whispers of passion
And the white rose breathes of love;
O, the red rose is a falcon,
And the white rose it a dove.

J.B.O'REILLY

I remember I remember
The roses red and white
Those flowers made of light.

THOMAS HOOD

Yoki San
Precious Platinum

Ah, see the Virgin Rose,
how sweetly she
Doth first peep forth with
bashful modesty,
That fairer seems the less
ye see her way!
Lo! See soon after,
how more bold and free
Her bared bosom she doth
broad display;
Lo! See soon after, how she
fades away and falls.

EDMUND SPENCER

Mischief

Lovliest of lovely things are they.
On earth that soonest pass away,
The rose that lives its little hour,
Is prized beyond the sculptured flower.

WILLIAM CULLEN

Dortmund

I haven't much time to be fond
of anything
but when I have a moment's
fondness to bestow
Most times the roses get it.

WILKIE COLLINS 1824-1889

Santa Fe

A sepal, petal and thorn
Upon a common summers morn
A flash of dew - a bee or two -
A breeze - a caper in the trees -
And I'm a rose!

EMILY DICKINSON 1830 - 1886

Apricot Nectar

Don't complain
that your roses have thorns
Just be grateful
that your thorns have Roses.

Sea Foam (weeping standard)
Iceberg

Perhaps few people have ever asked themselves why they admire a rose so much more than all other flowers. If they consider, they will find, first, that red is, in a delicately graduated state, the loveliness of all pure colours; and secondly, that in the rose there is no shadow, except which is composed of colour. All its shadows are fuller in colour than its lights, owing to the translucency and reflective power of its leaves.

JOHN RUSKIN

Santa Fe

Two roses on one slender spray
In sweet communion grew,
Together hailed the morning ray
And drank the evening dew.

JAMES MONTGOMERY

Autumn Delight

Then in that party,
all those powers
voted the rose
the queen of flowers.

ROBERT HERRICK

Queen Elizabeth

I wonder,
I wonder if anyone knows,
who lives in the heart
of this velvety rose,
now is it a goblin,
or is it an elf,
or is it the Queen
of the fairies herself.

All Gold

The price of a rose
is in a catalogue,
but the value of the rose
is in one's heart.

Cafe

I wish
the sky would rain down roses,
as they rain from off the shaken bush.
Why will it not?
Then all the valleys would be
pink and white,
and soft to tread on.

GEORGE ELLIOT 1819 - 1880

Queen Elizabeth
Iceberg

My solace I find in my roses,
Their perfection of colour and form,
Their fragrant appeal and their beauty,
Make one's outlook more peaceful and warm.

Iceberg

The rose is sweetest washed with
morning dew,
And love is loveliest when
embalmed in tears.

WALTER SCOTT

Santa Fe

Some prefer the Tea Rose
And some the Floribunda
Others choose the miniature
Over which to muse and wonder,
If the rambler, shrub, or climber,
Is best of all the roses.
But does it really matter
When guided by our noses.

JOE SHORTHAND

Dupontii

And the rose herself has got
Perfume which on earth is not.

JOHN KEATS

Was it not fate than, on this
July midnight -
Was it not fate
(whose name is also sorrow)
That bade me pause before the
Garden Gate.
To breathe the incense of those
slumbering roses?

EDGAR ALLEN POE

Dearest

As rich and purposeless
as is the rose;
The simple doom
is to be beautiful.

STEPHEN PHILLIPS

Diamond Jubilee

One Red Rose

On the estate of Overponds,
at Shackleford in Surrey,
there is a cottage which is held
on an interesting lease
for a thousand years
from the thirty-first year
of Queen Elizabeth 1 reign,
at the yearly rent of

one red Rose.

Precious Platinum

The End